Fern Green
photographs by Deirdre Rooney

hardie grant books

CONTENTS

INTRODUCTION

Energy balls and bars are the number one snack. They are full of amazing ingredients and are easy to make at home. Most of these recipes are dairy-free, gluten-free, and packed full of protein. The ingredients are rich in vitamins and minerals and can help boost the immune system, as well as having anti-inflammatory properties. Each one helps to boost your body's natural defences, giving it the protein it needs to function at its very best.

These energising snacks are easy to grab on the go, as they can be packed in a lunchbox for work, school, travel or workouts. You won't find any refined sugar in them, so they won't cause spikes in energy levels, just a consistent energy flow. They will also keep you feeling fuller for longer while giving you a boost in vitality and well-being. What more could you ask for in a little snack?

Shop-bought versus home-made

Making your own energy bars could not be easier, but if you have been tempted to buy them in the past, here are a few reasons why you might think again.

 Hydrogenated oils
These are bad fats that should be avoided. They increase the accumulation of body fat, which defeats the purpose of energy bars. They are found in shop-bought baked and deep-fried foods.

 Soy protein isolate (SPI)
Even though it says soy, it doesn't necessarily mean it is a good source of protein. In fact, SPI is a by-product of soy processing and some consider it to be a 'waste' product of this process.

 Artificial sweeteners
These help to improve flavour in shop-bought products, but they are digested quickly and may result in a blood sugar spike, which can lead to insulin resistance and increased appetite.

 High sugar
A lot of shop-bought bars contain over 20 g of sugar. Excess sugar means excessive amounts of calories, which makes you gain more weight instead of lean muscle.

However, there are some commercial energy bars available that are good for your health, so make sure you read the label to check the ingredients.

HELPFUL INGREDIENT TIPS

There is such a wide range of ingredients that you can use when making these energy snacks. Here are a few useful ingredient suggestions along with valuable hints and essential budget recommendations.

Organic coconut oil is used in many of the following recipes. Try to buy a large jar to save money and store it in the cupboard. Bear in mind that coconut oil liquefies at around 21°C/32°F.

Nuts and seeds can be expensive when buying small packets, so try to buy these in bulk, either online or at a local shop. This can reduce the cost dramatically. Store nuts and seeds in the cupboard in large airtight jars.

Medjool dates are used in a lot of these recipes instead of chopped or other dates. They are sold whole and are moister than chopped dates giving them a greater sticking power. Try to find these in bulk too.

Natural nut butters are used in some recipes. Some commercially made peanut butters contain a lot of oil, sugar, salt and preservatives to give them a creamy, whipped consistency and an artificial flavour, so make sure you check the label carefully before buying.

If you suffer from a nut allergy, you can replace the nut butter with seed butter in all these recipes. For example, sunflower seed and pumpkin seed butters are good alternatives.

BAKED & NON-BAKED

There are two types of bars to make at home, and one type of ball.

Baked

Baked bars tend to make a stronger crunchier bar, which maintains a longer shelf life. They keep their freshness, and are more likely to keep their shape. This makes them ideal for packed lunches or taking them on a run. Store them in an airtight container and perhaps wrap each bar in parchment or baking paper. Most recipes can last for up to a week in the fridge. Energy balls tend not to be baked due to their shape.

Non-baked

These bars and balls are not cooked. It is sometimes better to keep ingredients fresh, and leaving them for 15–60 minutes in the fridge helps them to become firm. With this method, the ingredients retain their texture and the fibre content of the fruits and nuts is preserved. This is why recipes with more of these fibrous ingredients in them are better uncooked, giving the bar or ball a satisfying chewiness. Store them in the fridge for up to 3 days. It is good to freeze them wrapped in parchment paper and then cling film, and only take them out when needed. Make sure the bar or ball has defrosted before eating.

Useful Equipment

Food processor – this is very helpful as it makes energy balls and bars even quicker and easier to prepare. You can use a pestle and mortar to grind up the nuts and seeds, but if you have a food processor you can whizz the ingredients up in seconds.

Square silicone tin or 20 x 20 cm baking tin – these are perfect for making bars. If making baked energy bars ensure the baking tin is lined with parchment paper before using. A silicone tin is also good as it saves the hassle of lining a tin when making non-baked bars.

Digital scale – helpful for measuring the ingredients.

CREATING YOUR OWN ENERGY BARS & BALLS

There are many ways to combine ingredients to make the perfect energy ball or bar. This is just a simple guide to create your very own, and help you get started.

Depending on what's in your cupboard, choose a mix of nuts and seeds. To help bind it together pick your favourite dried fruit, from large figs to small raisins. Then add optional ingredients from superfood powders to natural sweeteners and toppings. These can be whatever you like, so experiment and come up with your very own healthy protein boosting snack.

Nuts 125 g	+	Dried Fruit 250 g	+	Powders 1–2 teaspoons	+	Natural Sweeteners 1 tablespoon	+	Toppings
almonds		blueberries		acai		agave		cacao
cashews		cranberries		maca		coconut oil		coconut
hazelnuts		dates		matcha		honey		crushed nuts
pecans		figs				fruit purée		crushed seeds
walnuts		raisins				tahini		powders

1. Pick one item from each category, pop in a food processor and whizz to a paste.

2. Wet your hands, roll the mixture into balls or push into a lined baking tin. Roll in one of the topping ingredients or sprinkle on top, if using, and chill to firm up.

TOP 12 INGREDIENTS

Here is a list of the top superfood ingredients to make those delicious energy balls and bars taste great. They are all incredibly good for you and full of nutrients that make you feel better from within.

1. Chia seeds These are loaded with omega-3 fatty acids and are higher in calcium than cow's milk. They are also rich in antioxidants, anti-inflammatories and fibre.

2. Sesame seeds Black or white, these little seeds are full of vitamins and minerals, which help keep the immune system in top shape.

3. Hemp seeds Grind these to make an alternative to nut butter if you are allergic to nuts. They are an excellent source of essential fatty acids including omega-3 and -6, as well as zinc, magnesium and calcium, which are all powerful anti-inflammatories.

4. Oats Sometimes ground to make oatmeal, oats are high in fibre, helping to lower cholesterol and leave you feeling energised for hours.

5. Quinoa This contains all the essential amino acids that our bodies need and is full of manganese, magnesium and phosphorus, which is vital for our wellbeing.

6. Almonds The best nut for vitamin E and great at making butters and milks. They are also high in calcium, which is good for bones and teeth.

7. Walnuts These contain the stress-busting hormone melatonin and are high in cholesterol lowering compounds.

8. Cacao A natural chocolate full of antioxidants and vitamins, which helps send feel-good messages to the brain.

9. Carob Similar to cacao, but a little lighter in flavour. It contains gallic acid that works well as an antibacterial and helps improve digestion and lower cholesterol.

10. Coconut oil This contains a rich source of lauric acid, which helps boost immunity and fight disease.

11. Goji berries These contain more beta-carotene than any other plant as well as being very high in iron.

12. Dates As well as being high in fibre, dates are high in B vitamins, which help in the metabolism of food and formation of new blood cells. They are also a rich source of minerals.

NO-BAKE ENERGY BARS

These simple recipes are full of nuts, seeds and dried fruit to give you a healthy boost of energy whenever you need it. Freeze or chill them so that they're ready and waiting for when you are on the go.

Peanut & Cacao • Peanut & Carob
Beetroot & Dark Chocolate • Almond & Raisin
Peanut & Honey • Coconut, Almond & Date
Cashew Granola • Blueberry
Strawberry & Almond • Almond & Vanilla
Fudgy Maca • Maca • Spiced Apple & Date
Cashew & Date • Apricot, Coconut & Cashew
Super Seedy • Peanut & Banana • Choccy Fig
Prune & Almond • Puffed Almond & Cranberry

PEANUT & CACAO

Makes: 16
Preparation: 15 minutes + 30 minutes chilling

YOU NEED

135 g rolled oats • 90 g whey protein powder
20 g puffed brown rice • 85 g natural peanut butter (see page 154)
85 ml honey (preferably raw) • 1 vanilla pod, split and scraped
2 tablespoons cacao nibs

Cacao contains a high amount of magnesium, which helps relax your muscles.

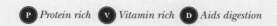 *Protein rich* *Vitamin rich* *Aids digestion*

Line a 20 × 20 cm baking tin. Blitz the oats in a food processor until fine. Mix with the whey powder and rice. Heat the peanut butter, honey, and vanilla seeds in a pan until melted, then add to the dry ingredients and mix well. Add the cacao nibs, stir, then press the mixture into the tin and chill until firm. Turn out of the tin and cut into 16 bars. Keep chilled.

PEANUT & CAROB

Makes: 16
Preparation: 15 minutes + 30 minutes chilling

YOU NEED
100 g puffed brown rice • 90 g oatmeal • 75 g carob chips
75 g unsweetened desiccated coconut • ¼ teaspoon ground cinnamon
70 g coconut oil, melted • 4 tablespoons natural peanut butter (see page 154)
60 ml brown rice syrup • ½ teaspoon vanilla extract

Carob contains gallic acid, which has antibacterial properties.

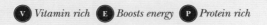

V *Vitamin rich* **E** *Boosts energy* **P** *Protein rich*

Line a 20 × 20 cm baking tin. Combine the rice, oatmeal, carob, coconut and cinnamon in a bowl. Combine the coconut oil, peanut butter, brown rice syrup and vanilla extract, then stir both mixtures together and press into the tin. Use the back of a spoon to level the top. Chill until firm. Turn out of the tin and cut into 16 squares. Keep chilled.

BEETROOT & DARK CHOCOLATE

Makes: 16
Preparation: 30 minutes + overnight chilling

YOU NEED

250 g beetroot, cooked and chopped • 5 tablespoons honey (preferably raw)
40 g rolled oats • 180 g strawberry-flavoured soy protein powder
30 g dried strawberries, chopped • 100 g dark chocolate chips

Beetroot contains tryptophan, which helps relax the mind and creates a sense of well-being.

V *Vitamin rich* **B** *Blood purifying* **E** *Boosts energy*

Line a 20 × 20 cm baking tin. Blend the beetroot and honey together in a food processor until smooth. Combine the oats, protein powder and strawberries and stir into the beetroot. Press into the tin. Melt the chocolate chips in a non-stick pan over a low heat, then spread over the top of the mixture. Chill overnight. Turn out of the tin and cut into 16 bars. Keep chilled.

ALMOND & RAISIN

Makes: 16
Preparation: 15 minutes + overnight chilling

YOU NEED

200 g rolled oats • 150 ml honey (preferably raw) • 90 ml unsweetened almond milk
3 tablespoons pure maple syrup • 100 g blanched almonds, chopped
1 teaspoon salt • 70 g raisins

These bars are high in fibre, which aids digestion.

B *Boosts bone health*   **I** *Boosts immunity*   **M** *Mineral rich*

Line a 20 × 20 cm baking tin. Mix the oats and honey together, then slowly add the almond milk and maple syrup. Add the almonds, salt and raisins and stir well. Press the mixture into the tin and chill overnight. Turn out of the tin and cut into 16 bars. Keep chilled.

PEANUT & HONEY

Makes: 16
Preparation: 20 minutes + 30 minutes freezing

YOU NEED

30 g golden flaxseeds • 90 g rolled oats • 50 g unsweetened desiccated coconut
180 ml honey (preferably raw) • 1 vanilla pod, split and scraped
130 g peanuts • 80 g raisins

Flaxseeds are the richest plant source of omega-3 fatty acids, which are essential to keep your brain, heart, joints and immune system healthy.

V *Vitamin rich*　**D** *Aids digestion*　**P** *Protein rich*

Line a 20 × 20 cm baking tin. Blend the flaxseeds, oats and desiccated coconut in a food processor. Transfer to a bowl and add the honey, vanilla seeds and peanuts. Stir well, then add the raisins. Press the mixture into the tin and freeze for 30 minutes. Turn out of the tin and cut into chunky bars. Keep chilled.

COCONUT, ALMOND & DATE

Makes: 16
Preparation: 20 minutes + 6 hours chilling

YOU NEED

150 g blanched almonds, toasted • 100 g walnuts • 150 g Medjool dates, pitted
60 g rice protein powder • 1 teaspoon salt • 180 ml light coconut milk
30 g puffed brown rice • 40 g raisins • 45 g unsweetened desiccated coconut
1 tablespoon coconut oil, melted

Almonds are a great source of calcium, magnesium and phosphorus.

 B *Body strengthening* M *Mineral rich* I *Boosts immunity*

Line a 20 × 20 cm square baking tin. Blend the nuts, dates, protein powder, salt and coconut milk in a food processor. Pour the mixture into a bowl and add the brown rice, raisins, dessicated coconut and coconut oil. Stir to combine, then press the mixture into the tin. Chill for up to 6 hours. Turn out of the tin and cut into 16 bars. Keep chilled.

CASHEW GRANOLA

Makes: 16
Preparation: 15 minutes + 1 hour freezing

YOU NEED

120 g rolled oats • ½ teaspoon salt • 5 tablespoons honey (preferably raw)
120 g cashew butter (see page 154) • 70 g whey protein powder • 30 g raisins

Cashews contain minerals, zinc, copper and iron.

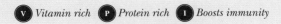 Vitamin rich Protein rich Boosts immunity

Line a 20 × 20 cm baking tin. Mix the oats, salt and honey together in a bowl. Whisk the cashew butter and protein powder together in another bowl and add to the oat mixture. Stir in the raisins, then press the mixture into the tin. Freeze for 1 hour. Turn out of the tin and cut into 16 squares. Keep chilled.

BLUEBERRY

Makes: 16
Preparation: 20 minutes + overnight chilling

YOU NEED

120 g rolled oats • 70 g whey protein powder • 5 tablespoons honey (preferably raw)
120 g edible cocoa butter • ½ tablespoon salt • 50 g blueberries

Blueberries are a good source of vitamin K.

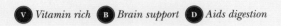 *Vitamin rich*  *Brain support* *Aids digestion*

Line a 20 × 20 cm baking tin. Blend the oats in a food processor until they are a fine powder. Pour into a bowl and add the protein powder. Heat the honey, cocoa butter, salt and blueberries in a pan over a medium heat and pour over the protein mixture. Mix well, then press the mixture into the tin. Chill overnight. Turn out of the tin and cut into 16 bars. Keep chilled.

STRAWBERRY & ALMOND

Makes: 16
Preparation: 20 minutes + 2 hours chilling

YOU NEED

130 g blanched almonds, toasted and chopped • 30 g hemp seeds
180 ml honey (preferably raw) • 120 g rice protein powder • 60 g dried strawberries

Hemp seeds are an excellent source of essential fatty acids including omega-3 and -6.

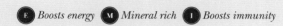 *Boosts energy* ● *Mineral rich* ● *Boosts immunity*

Line a 20 × 20 cm baking tin. Mix the nuts and seeds together in a bowl, then pour over the honey. Stir in the protein powder. Fold in the dried strawberries and press the mixture into the tin. Chill for 2 hours. Turn out of the tin and cut into 16 squares. Keep chilled.

ALMOND & VANILLA

Makes: 16
Preparation: 20 minutes + 30 minutes freezing

YOU NEED

100 g oatmeal • 50 g rolled oats • 40 g vanilla whey protein powder

3 tablespoons puffed brown rice • 110 ml honey (preferably raw)

100 g almond butter (see page 154) • 1 vanilla pod, split and scraped

60 g carob chips

Oats have a very high fibre content and help remove cholesterol from the digestive system.

 Mineral rich  Aids digestion  Protein rich

Line a 20 × 20 cm baking tin. Combine the oatmeal, oats, whey protein and brown rice in a bowl. Heat the honey, almond butter and vanilla seeds in a saucepan until melted together, then add to the dry ingredients and stir in the carob chips. Press the mixture into a tin and freeze for 30 minutes. Turn out of the tin and cut into 16 bars. Keep chilled.

FUDGY MACA

Makes: 12–16
Preparation: 10 minutes + 30 minutes soaking & 30 minutes freezing

YOU NEED

110 g chia seeds • 30 g hemp seeds • 230 ml unsweetened almond milk
80 g cacao nibs • 75 g almond butter (see page 154)
60 g coconut oil, melted • 4 tablespoons honey (preferably raw)
2 tablespoons maca powder • pinch of salt
freeze-dried raspberries, for topping

Maca powder is high in vitamin B6, calcium and iron. It is also a good source of thiamin and protein.

B *Blood building*   **E** *Boosts energy*   **H** *Balances hormones*

Line a 20 × 20 cm square baking tin. Soak the chia and hemp seeds in the almond milk for 30 minutes. Blend all of the ingredients in a food processor until they form a thick batter. Pour into the tin and press down to 4–5 cm in height. Sprinkle the raspberries over the top. Freeze for 30 minutes until firm, then turn out of the tin and cut into 12–16 bars. Chill for up to 2 weeks.

MACA

Makes: 8–10
Preparation: 12 minutes + 1 hour chilling

YOU NEED

150 g blanched almonds • ½ teaspoon salt • 70 g sunflower seeds
65 g pumpkin seeds • 2 tablespoons chia seeds • 2 tablespoons maca powder
80 g ground flaxseeds • 65 ml pure maple syrup
35 g almond butter (see page 154) • 65 ml coconut oil, melted

Maca powder is great for balancing your mood.

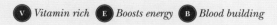

Vitamin rich *Boosts energy* *Blood building*

Line a 20 × 20 cm baking tin. Pulse the almonds in a food processor until they reach
a coarse consistency. Put into a bowl with the salt, sunflower seeds, pumpkin seeds,
chia seeds, maca powder and flaxseeds. Melt the maple syrup, almond butter and oil
in a pan for 3 minutes. Pour over the seeds and mix well. Press the mixture into the
tin and chill for 1 hour. Turn out of the tin and cut into 8–10 squares.
Keep chilled.

SPICED APPLE & DATE

Makes: 16
Preparation: 20 minutes + 30 minutes chilling

YOU NEED

150 g cashews • 100 g Medjool dates, pitted and chopped

1 teaspoon ground cinnamon • ¼ teaspoon nutmeg, grated

2 tablespoons Date Purée (see page 152) • 90 g rolled oats • 160 g wholemeal flour

2 tablespoons hemp seeds • 30 g sunflower seeds • 30 g unsweetened desiccated coconut

2 tablespoons cashew butter (see page 154) • 75 ml pure maple syrup

70 g dried apples, chopped

Cashews are high in copper, which is vital for energy production.

Line a 20 × 20 cm baking tin. Blitz the cashews, dates, cinnamon, nutmeg and date purée in a food processor for 30 seconds. Transfer to a bowl. Add the oats, flour, hemp seeds, sunflower seeds and coconut and stir well. Melt the cashew butter and maple syrup in a pan until combined. Pour over the dry ingredients and add the dried apples. Stir, then press the mixture into the tin. Chill until cool. Turn out of the tin and cut into 16 bars. Keep chilled.

CASHEW & DATE

Makes: 16
Preparation: 10 minutes + 2 hours chilling

YOU NEED
600 g cashews • 500 g Medjool dates, pitted

Dates are loaded with fibre, which is great for lowering cholesterol.

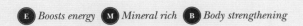

E *Boosts energy* **M** *Mineral rich* **B** *Body strengthening*

Line a 20 × 20 cm baking tin. Blitz the cashews and dates in a food processor until they become a fine consistency. Pour the mixture into a tin, press down, cover with cling film and chill for about 2 hours, or until firm. Turn out of the tin and cut into 16 squares. Keep chilled.

APRICOT, COCONUT & CASHEW

Makes: 16
Preparation: 20 minutes + 2 hours freezing

YOU NEED

80 g cashews • 150 g Medjool dates, pitted • 12 dried apricots

2 tablespoons ground flaxseeds • 150 g grated fresh coconut

Dried apricots are high in dietary fibre, which in turn helps digestion.

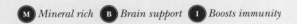 *Mineral rich* *Brain support* *Boosts immunity*

Line a 20 × 20 cm baking tin. Blitz the cashews in a food processor until finely chopped. Set aside. Pulse the dates and apricots in the food processor until well chopped. Add the cashews and pulse again. Mix the flaxseeds with 65 ml water in a small bowl. Tip into the food processor and pulse until a sticky ball is formed. Spread the sticky ball over the base of the tin. Sprinkle fresh coconut over the top. Cover with cling film and freeze for 2 hours, or until hardened. Turn out of the tin and cut into 16 bars. Freeze until ready to serve. Defrost until soft enough to eat.

SUPER SEEDY

Makes: 12–16
Preparation: 20 minutes + 30 minutes chilling

YOU NEED

100 g puffed wheat or puffed brown rice • 75 g rolled oats • 3 tablespoons sunflower seeds

75 g oat bran • ½ tablespoon poppy seeds • 3 tablespoons hemp seeds

150 g Medjool dates, pitted and chopped • 3 tablespoons almond butter (see page 154)

80 g cacao powder • 60 ml honey (preferably raw) • ½ teaspoon vanilla extract

3 tablespoons dried cranberries, chopped • 2 tablespoons unsweetened desiccated coconut

Hemp seeds are an excellent source of essential fatty acids including omega-3 and -6.

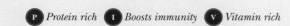

P *Protein rich*　**I** *Boosts immunity*　**V** *Vitamin rich*

Line a 20 × 20 cm baking tin. Pulse the wheat, oats, sunflower seeds, oat bran, poppy seeds and hemp seeds in a food processor for 5 minutes, then place in a bowl. Process the dates with 5 tablespoons of warm water to make a paste and add to the bowl. Heat the almond butter, cacao powder and honey in a pan until warm and slightly runny. Stir in the vanilla and add to the date mixture. Add the cranberries and coconut and mix. Spread the mixture into the tin. Chill until cool. Turn out of the tin and cut into 12–16 bars. Keep chilled.

PEANUT & BANANA

Makes: 16
Preparation: 15 minutes + 30 minutes freezing

YOU NEED

2 ripe bananas, mashed • 200 g raisins • 1 teaspoon vanilla extract
300 g rolled oats • 60 g fresh coconut • 120 g sunflower seeds, toasted
120 g spelt flour • 75 g roasted unsalted peanuts, chopped
2 tablespoons coconut oil, melted • 3 tablespoons natural peanut butter (see page 154)
2 tablespoons honey (preferably raw)

Bananas are high in potassium, which is good for nerve and muscle function.

B *Brain support*   **B** *Body strengthening*   **B** *Blood building*

Line a 20 × 20 cm baking tin. Pulse the bananas, raisins and vanilla in a food processor for 30 seconds. Add the oats, coconut and sunflower seeds and pulse for another 30 seconds, then pour into a bowl. Stir in the flour and peanuts and set aside. Heat the oil, peanut butter and honey in a small pan until warm. Pour over the oat mixture and combine well. Press into the tin and freeze for 30 minutes. Turn out of the tin and cut into 16 bars. Keep chilled.

CHOCCY FIG

Makes: 16
Preparation: 10 minutes + 30 minutes chilling

YOU NEED

200 g dried figs • 100 g Medjool dates, pitted

200 g blanched almonds • 150 g rolled oats

3 tablespoons Date Purée (see page 152)

2 tablespoons cacao powder • ¼ teaspoon almond extract

Figs are a great source of calcium, which keeps bones healthy.

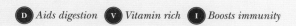 **D** *Aids digestion* **V** *Vitamin rich* **I** *Boosts immunity*

Line a 20 × 20 cm baking tin. Blitz all of the ingredients in a food processor until finely ground. Press into the tin and chill until firm. Turn out of the tin and cut into 16 bars. Keep chilled.

PRUNE & ALMOND

Makes: 16
Preparation: 10 minutes + 30 minutes chilling

YOU NEED

250 g prunes, pitted • 150 g blanched almonds • 4 tablespoons cacao powder
4 tablespoons almond butter (see page 154) • 4 tablespoons honey (preferably raw)

Prunes are a good source of potassium, copper, boron and magnesium.

H *Boosts heart health* **D** *Aids digestion* **V** *Vitamin rich*

Line a 20 × 20 cm baking tin. Blitz all of the ingredients in a food processor until fine.
Press into the tin and chill until firm. Turn out of the tin and cut into 16 squares.
Keep chilled.

PUFFED ALMOND & CRANBERRY

Makes: 16
Preparation: 15 minutes + 30 minutes chilling

YOU NEED

100 g puffed brown rice • 90 g oatmeal • 75 g dried cranberries
75 g blanched almonds, chopped • ¼ teaspoon ground cinnamon
70 g coconut oil, melted • 4 tablespoons almond butter (see page 154)
60 ml brown rice syrup • ½ teaspoon vanilla extract

Almonds can give you an energy boost, so these bars make an ideal snack.

V *Vitamin rich* E *Boosts energy* P *Protein rich*

Line a 20 × 20 cm baking tin. Combine the rice, oatmeal, cranberries, chopped almonds and cinnamon in a bowl. In another bowl, combine the oil, almond butter, brown rice syrup and vanilla extract. Mix both mixtures together and press into the tin. Chill for 30 minutes until firm. Turn out of the tin and cut into 16 bars. Keep chilled.

BAKED ENERGY BARS

These quick recipes are full of protein-rich ingredients to give you a nourishing energy boost. All the bars are simple to prepare and easy to wrap and take with you, wherever you are going during the day.

Cinnamon & Carrot • Yoghurt & Oat
Banana & Flaxseed • Lemon & Honey
Apple & Date • Pumpkin & Coconut.
Dried Berries • Quinoa & Date
Almond & Raspberry • Almond • Cherry
Pumpkin & Goji • Banana & Hemp • Chocolate
& Black Bean • Chickpea & Pineapple • Spiced
Apple & Almond • Honey Granola
Toasted Almond • Nut & Seed Crunch
Breakfast Chia

CINNAMON & CARROT

Makes: 12–16
Preparation: 10 minutes   Cooking: 25 minutes

YOU NEED

130 g egg whites • 230 g carrots, puréed • 120 g porridge oats
60 g vanilla whey protein powder • ½ teaspoon bicarbonate of soda
120 ml pure maple syrup • ½ teaspoon ground cinnamon

Carrots are high in fibre and beta-carotene. They are also a rich source of vitamin C, which helps boost the immune system.

V *Vitamin rich* **P** *Protein rich* **I** *Boosts immunity*

Preheat the oven to 180°C (350°F/Gas 4). Line a 20 × 20 cm baking tin. In a bowl, whisk the egg whites and carrot purée together. Sift the porridge oats and whey protein over another bowl, then add the bicarbonate of soda, syrup and cinnamon. Combine the wet and dry ingredients, then pour into the tin and bake for 25 minutes. Cool before cutting into 12–16 bars. Store in an airtight container for up to 4 days or chill for up to a week.

YOGHURT & OAT

Makes: 6
Preparation: 10 minutes   Cooking: 15 minutes

YOU NEED

240 g plain Greek yoghurt • 60 g whey protein powder
90 g rolled oats • 3 tablespoons honey (preferably raw)

Yoghurt contains lots of healthy bacteria, which is good for the digestive system.

B *Boosts bone health*   **P** *Protein rich*   **V** *Vitamin rich*

Preheat the oven to 180°C (350°F/Gas 4). Line a 20 cm loaf tin. Mix the yoghurt, protein powder and oats together and press into the tin. Spread the honey on top and bake for 15 minutes. Cool. Cut into 6 chunky bars. Store in an airtight container for up to 4 days or chill for a week.

BANANA & FLAXSEED

Makes: 12–16
Preparation: 10 minutes   Cooking: 15 minutes

YOU NEED
180 g rolled oats • 120 g whey protein powder
2 teaspoons golden flaxseeds • 200 g almond butter (see page 154)
180 ml Date Purée (see page 152) • 5 tablespoons honey (preferably raw)
2 ripe bananas, mashed • 1 teaspoon vanilla extract

Oats are rich in a dietary fibre called beta-glucan, which helps lower levels of bad cholesterol.

P *Protein rich* **M** *Mineral rich* **I** *Boosts immunity*

Preheat the oven to 180°C (350°F/Gas 4). Line a 20 × 20 cm baking tin. Mix all of the ingredients together in a bowl until combined. Press the mixture into the tin and bake for 15 minutes. Cool, then cut into 12–16 bars. Store in an airtight container for up to 4 days or chill for up to one week.

LEMON & HONEY

Makes: 12–16
Preparation: 10 minutes   Cooking: 25 minutes

YOU NEED

60 g porridge oats • 30 g vanilla whey protein powder • ½ teaspoon salt
½ teaspoon baking powder • zest of 1 lemon
150 ml honey (preferably raw) • 60 g egg whites • juice of ½ lemon
180 ml Date Purée (see page 152)

Lemon helps cleanse the liver, and has strong antibacterial properties.

V Vitamin rich P Protein rich D Aids digestion

Preheat the oven to 180°C (350°F/Gas 4). Line a 20 × 20 cm baking tin. Sift the porridge oats, protein powder, salt and baking powder into a bowl. Stir in the lemon zest and all of the wet ingredients. Add 230 ml water, stir until well combined, then pour the mixture into the tin. Bake for 25 minutes. Cool, then cut into 12–16 bars. Store in an airtight container for 4 days or chill for a week.

APPLE & DATE

Makes: 12–16
Preparation: 25 minutes   Cooking: 50 minutes

YOU NEED

3 apples, peeled, cored and grated • 120 ml apple juice

180 g Medjool dates, pitted and chopped • 60 ml coconut oil, melted

2 tablespoons agave nectar • 125 g rolled oats • 50 g wholemeal flour

1 teaspoon ground cinnamon • 2 tablespoons sesame seeds • 60 g walnuts

Dates are high in fibre and B vitamins, which helps balance the metabolism.

V *Vitamin rich* **I** *Boosts immunity* **D** *Aids digestion*

Preheat the oven to 180°C (350°F/Gas 4). Line a 20 × 20 cm baking tin. Combine
the apples, apple juice, half of the dates, oil and agave nectar. Stir in the oats, flour,
cinnamon, sesame seeds, nuts and the remaining dates. Leave for 10 minutes. Press
the mixture into the tin. Bake for 50 minutes. Cut into bars while warm, then cool in
the tin. Store in an airtight container for up to 4 days or chill for up to one week.

PUMPKIN & COCONUT

Makes: 12–16
Preparation: 30 minutes   Cooking: 15 minutes

YOU NEED

2 medium eggs • 170 g Pumpkin Purée (see page 156)

30 g almond butter (see page 154) • 40 g coconut flour

1½ teaspoons bicarbonate of soda • 60 g rice protein powder

a pinch of ground cinnamon • 40 g arrowroot • 50 g coconut oil, melted

For the icing

70 g almond butter • 70 g coconut butter • 90 ml coconut milk

4 teaspoons honey (preferably raw)

Eggs are a rich source of selenium, vitamins D, B6 and B12, plus zinc, iron and copper.

P *Protein rich* **V** *Vitamin rich* **E** *Boosts energy*

Preheat the oven to 180°C (350°F/Gas 4). Line a 20 × 20 cm baking tin. Combine the eggs, pumpkin and nut butter in a bowl and mix until smooth. Sift the flours, the bicarbonate of soda, protein powder, cinnamon and arrowroot into bowl. Add the oil and stir well. Press the mixture into the tin and bake for 15 minutes, then cool. Combine all of the icing ingredients, then spread over the baked mixture. Cut into 12–16 squares. Store in an airtight container for up to 4 days or chill for up to a week.

DRIED BERRIES

Makes: 12–16
Preparation: 10 minutes   Cooking: 30 minutes

YOU NEED

120 g vanilla whey protein powder • 125 g porridge oats

30 g dried cranberries, blueberries and raspberries, chopped

½ teaspoon salt • 1 teaspoon baking powder • juice of 1 lemon

90 g egg whites • 210 ml Date Purée (see page 152) • 90 ml honey (preferably raw)

Berries are high in dietary fibre and antioxidants.

Preheat the oven to 180°C (350°F/Gas 4). Line a 20 × 20 cm baking tin. Combine the whey protein, oats, berries, salt and baking powder. Mix in the lemon juice, egg whites, date purée, honey and 120 ml water. Stir, then press the mixture into the tin and bake for 30 minutes. Cool, then cut into 12–16 bars. Store in an airtight container for up to 4 days or chill for up to a week.

QUINOA & DATE

Makes: 16
Preparation: 15 minutes   Cooking: 25 minutes

YOU NEED

30 g golden flaxseeds • 30 g fresh coconut, grated • 60 g rice protein powder
60 g ground almonds • 400 g red quinoa, cooked
100 g Medjool dates, pitted • 50 g carob chips

Quinoa is rich in magnesium, manganese, copper, iron and phosphorus.

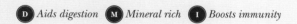 *Aids digestion* *Mineral rich* *Boosts immunity*

Preheat the oven to 180°C (350°F/Gas 4). Line a 20 × 20 cm baking tin. Blend the flaxseeds and coconut in a food processor. Add the protein powder and ground almonds and blend for 10 seconds. Tip in the quinoa and dates and blend until it holds together. Put into a bowl and stir in the carob chips. Press evenly into the tin and bake for 25 minutes. Cool, then cut into 16 squares. Store in an airtight container for up to 4 days or chill for up to a week.

ALMOND & RASPBERRY

Makes: 16
Preparation: 45 minutes   Cooking: 27 minutes

YOU NEED

For the base

120 g ground almonds • 2 tablespoons coconut oil, melted • 1 tablespoon water
pinch of salt

For the filling

150 g frozen raspberries • 90 ml pure maple syrup • 1 vanilla pod, seeds removed

For the topping

120 g walnuts • 80 g fresh coconut • 90 ml pure maple syrup
4 tablespoons coconut oil, melted • pinch of salt

Almonds are a good source of calcium, which is great for keeping bones and teeth healthy.

P *Protein rich* **D** *Aids digestion* **I** *Boosts immunity*

Simmer all of the filling ingredients in a pan for 10 minutes. Preheat the oven to 180°C (350°F/Gas 4). Line a 20 × 20 cm baking tin. Blend all of the base ingredients in a food processor. Press into the tin and bake for 12 minutes. Blend all of the topping ingredients in the food processor, keeping a coarse texture. Spread the filling over the base, then spread the topping mixture on top. Bake for 15 minutes. Cool. Cut into 16 bars. Store for up to 4 days or chill for up to a week.

ALMOND

Makes: 16

Preparation: 15 minutes   Cooking: 15 minutes

YOU NEED

100 g edible cocoa butter • ½ teaspoon salt • 3 tablespoons pure maple syrup

115 ml honey (preferably raw) • 240 ml unsweetened almond milk

100 g blanched almonds, chopped • 250 g porridge oats

Almonds are a great source of calcium.

M *Mineral rich* **I** *Boosts immunity* **D** *Aids digestion*

Preheat the oven to 180°C (350°F/Gas 4). Line a 20 × 20 cm baking tin. Simmer the cocoa butter, salt, maple syrup, honey and almond milk in a pan until melted. Keep stirring and let the mixture cool before adding the almonds and oats. Mix, then press into the tin. Bake for 15 minutes. Cool. Cut into 16 bars. Store in an airtight container for up to 4 days or chill for up to a week.

CHERRY

Makes: 12
Preparation: 15 minutes   Cooking: 30–35 minutes

YOU NEED
150 g blanched almonds, chopped • 90 g rolled oats • 60 g whey protein powder
30 g sunflower seeds • 50 g cherries, stoned and chopped
2 apples, peeled, cored and grated • 2 teaspoons egg whites
30 g cashews, chopped

Cherries contain powerful antioxidants and are high in fibre and vitamin C.

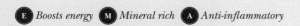 **E** *Boosts energy* **M** *Mineral rich* **A** *Anti-inflammatory*

Preheat the oven to 180°C (350°F/Gas 4). Line a 20 × 20 cm baking tin. Put the almonds, oats, protein powder, seeds and cherries into a bowl and stir until well combined. Add the apples, egg whites and cashews and stir well. Press the mixture into the tin and bake for 30–35 minutes. Cool. Cut into 12 bars. Store in an airtight container for up to 4 days or chill for up to a week.

PUMPKIN & GOJI

Makes: 12–16
Preparation: 10 minutes   Cooking: 25–30 minutes

YOU NEED

50 g flaked almonds • 65 g pumpkin seeds • 85 g rolled oats
½ teaspoon bicarbonate of soda • ½ teaspoon ground cinnamon
½ teaspoon allspice • 50 g goji berries • 80 ml brown rice syrup
80 ml molasses or black treacle •110 g Pumpkin Purée (see page 156)
1 teaspoon vanilla extract

Goji berries are rich in iron, calcium and protein.

(M) *Mineral rich* (B) *Brain support* (P) *Protein rich*

Preheat the oven to 180°C (350°F/Gas 4). Line a 20 × 20 cm baking tin. Put the almonds, pumpkin seeds and oats onto a baking tray and bake until golden. Transfer into a bowl and stir in the bicarbonate of soda and spices. Pour boiling water over the goji berries to soften. Drain, then add to the mixture. Mix well. Heat the rice syrup and molasses then, when melted, add the pumpkin purée and vanilla and stir into the mixture. Stir, press into a tin and bake for 25–30 minutes. Cool. Cut into 12–16 squares. Store in an airtight container for up to 4 days or chill for up to a week.

BANANA & HEMP

Makes: 24
Preparation: 10 minutes   Cooking: 20 minutes

YOU NEED
175 g Medjool dates, pitted and chopped • 4 ripe bananas, mashed

170 g rolled oats • 65 g pumpkin seeds, roughly chopped

80 g hemp seeds, chopped a little in a food processor

1 teaspoon ground cinnamon • 2 teaspoons vanilla extract

Hemp is high in essential omega-6 fatty acids and gamma linolenic acid, also found in borage oil and egg yolks, which has been proven to naturally balance hormones.

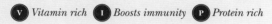

V *Vitamin rich* I *Boosts immunity* P *Protein rich*

Preheat the oven to 180°C (350°F/Gas 4). Line a 20 × 20 cm baking tin. Put all of the ingredients into a bowl and stir well. Press firmly into the tin and bake for 20 minutes. Cool, then cut into 24 squares. Store in an airtight container for up to 4 days or chill for up to a week.

CHOCOLATE & BLACK BEAN

Makes: 12–16
Preparation: 15 minutes   Cooking: 25 minutes

YOU NEED

45 g black beans, cooked • 25 g cashew butter (see page 154)
2 tablespoons brown rice syrup • 3 tablespoons date syrup
50 ml coconut oil, melted • ½ teaspoon vanilla extract • 75 g rolled oats
25 g porridge oats • 30 g cacao powder • ½ teaspoon baking powder
½ teaspoon ground cinnamon • 35 g sunflower seeds, chopped
25 g dried cranberries, chopped

Black beans are rich in phytonutrients and help to keep your digestive tract healthy.

B *Blood building*   **E** *Boosts energy*   **V** *Vitamin rich*

Preheat the oven to 180°C (350°F/Gas 4). Line a 20 × 20 cm baking tin. Whizz the beans, nut butter, rice and date syrups, oil and vanilla extract in a food processor until smooth. Put the oats, porridge oats, cacao, baking powder, cinnamon, sunflower seeds and cranberries in a bowl and mix. Add the bean mixture and stir until well combined. Press into the tin and bake for 25 minutes. Cool. Cut into 12–16 squares. Store in an airtight container for up to 4 days or chill for up to a week.

CHICKPEA & PINEAPPLE

Makes: 12–16
Preparation: 10 minutes   Cooking: 20 minutes

YOU NEED

150 g blanched almonds • 55 g canned chickpeas, drained

2 tablespoons agave nectar • 2 tablespoons coconut oil, melted

45 g Medjool dates, pitted and chopped

5 g dried pineapple, chopped • 45 g dried papaya, chopped

2 tablespoons pineapple juice • 25 g unsweetened desiccated coconut

200 g porridge oats • 150 g wholemeal flour

Chickpeas are high in protein and a great source of manganese and folate.

P *Protein rich*   **B** *Body strengthening*   **V** *Vitamin rich*

Preheat the oven to 180°C (350°F/Gas 4). Line a 20 × 20 cm baking tin. Pulse the almonds in a food processor until fine. Add the chickpeas, 80 ml water, agave nectar, oil, dates, pineapple, papaya and pineapple juice and process until combined. Mix the coconut, oats and flour together in a bowl, then add the chickpea mixture. Stir well and press into the tin. Bake for 20 minutes. Cool. Cut into 12–16 bars. Store in an airtight container for up to 4 days or chill for up to a week.

SPICED APPLE & ALMOND

Makes: 12
Preparation: 15 minutes   Cooking: 25 minutes

YOU NEED

120 g rice protein powder • ½ teaspoon salt • 2 teaspoons baking powder

1 teaspoon grated nutmeg • 2 teaspoons ground cinnamon • 65 g ground almonds

100 g fat-free cottage cheese • 1 teaspoon vanilla extract

90 ml pure maple syrup • 3 egg whites

1 apple, peeled, cored and grated

This is a filling protein bar, which helps stave off those hunger pangs.

E *Boosts energy* **V** *Vitamin rich* **D** *Aids digestion*

Preheat the oven to 180°C (350°F/Gas 4). Line a 20 × 20 cm baking tin. Sift the
protein powder, salt, baking powder, nutmeg, cinnamon into a bowl and stir in the
almonds. In another bowl, whisk the cottage cheese, vanilla extract, maple syrup and
egg whites until frothy, then add to the almond mix. Add the grated apple and stir
well. Press the mixture into the tin and bake for 25 minutes. Cool. Cut into 12 bars.
Store in an airtight container for up to 4 days or chill for up to a week.

HONEY GRANOLA

Makes: 12–16
Preparation: 10 minutes   Cooking: 20 minutes

YOU NEED

85 g rolled oats • 30 g wheatgerm • 55 g ground flaxseeds

60 g unsweetened desiccated coconut • 45 g pumpkin seeds, toasted

50 g sesame seeds, toasted • 50 g flaked almonds, toasted

125 g Medjool dates, pitted and chopped • 30 g dried cranberries, chopped

230 g honey (preferably raw) • 1 tablespoon coconut oil, melted

Flaxseed is a rich source of dietary fibre, manganese, vitamin B1 and omega-3 fatty acids.

V *Vitamin rich* **D** *Aids digestion* **P** *Protein rich*

Preheat the oven to 180°C (350°F/Gas 4). Line a 20 × 20 cm baking tin. Combine the oats, wheatgerm, flaxseeds, coconut, pumpkin seeds, sesame seeds, almonds, dates and cranberries. Heat the honey and oil until runny, then add to the dry ingredients. Press the mixture into the tin and bake for 20 minutes. Cool, then cut into 12–16 bars. Store in airtight container for up to 4 days or chill for up to a week.

TOASTED ALMOND

Makes: 12–16
Preparation: 10 minutes   Cooking: 20 minutes

YOU NEED
450 g flaked almonds, toasted • 170 g brown rice syrup

Almonds are a good source of calcium, magnesium and phosphorus.

P *Protein rich* **B** *Body strengthening* **E** *Boosts energy*

Preheat the oven to 180°C (350°F/Gas 4). Line a 20 × 20 cm baking tin. Put the almonds in a bowl and pour over the rice syrup. Mix well. Press into the tin and bake for 20 minutes until golden. Cool. Cut into 12–16 bars. Store in an airtight container for up to 4 days or chill for up to a week.

NUT & SEED CRUNCH

Makes: 12–16
Preparation: 10 minutes   Cooking: 20 minutes

YOU NEED

425 g salted peanuts, roasted • 140 g sunflower seeds, toasted

130 g pumpkin seeds, toasted • 35 g sesame seeds, toasted

40 g chia seeds • 220 g brown rice syrup

Chia seeds are an excellent source of omega-3 fatty acids, which help protect against heart attacks and strokes.

P *Protein rich* **M** *Mineral rich* **B** *Stabilises blood sugar*

Preheat the oven to 180°C (350°F/Gas 4). Line a 20 × 20 cm baking tin. Put the nuts and seeds into a bowl. Heat the rice syrup and pour over the nuts. Stir, then press into the tin. Bake for 20 minutes. Cool. Cut into 12–16 squares. Store in an airtight container for up to 4 days or chill for up to a week.

BREAKFAST CHIA

Makes: 12–16
Preparation: 5 minutes   Cooking: 25–30 minutes

YOU NEED
2 apples, peeled, cored and grated • 130 ml agave nectar
150 g coconut oil, melted • 170 g rolled oats • 80 g hazelnuts, chopped
4 tablespoons chia seeds • 2 tablespoons ground flaxseeds
3 tablespoons cacao nibs

Hazelnuts contain flavonoids, which help support brain health and improve circulation.

E *Boosts energy*   **V** *Vitamin rich*   **P** *Protein rich*

Preheat the oven to 190°C (375°F/Gas 5). Line a 20 × 20 cm baking tin. Combine all of the ingredients in a bowl and leave for 15 minutes until the oats have softened. Pour into the tin and bake for 25–30 minutes. Cool. Cut into 12–16 squares. Store for up to 4 days or chill for up to a week.

NO-BAKE ENERGY BALLS

These small balls of goodness are packed with protein to give you an energy boost whenever you need it. They taste delicious and are very quick to make — great for the whole family.

Tahini & Fig • Cranberry & Almond
Coconut & Cashew • The Ultimate
Blueberry Paleo • Cinnamon Apple • Cacao
Chia Coconut • Fig & Walnut • Almond & Carob
Cranberry & Orange • Spiced Pumpkin
Matcha Chocolate • Golden Sultana & Coconut
Date & Nut Butter • Almond & Quinoa • Lemon
Chia Cashew • Spiced Oats & Acai
Chia & Cherry • Apricot & Cashew • Coconut
Coconut & Date • Cranberry & Pomegranate
Lemon & Poppy Seed • Puffed Almond
Spiced Carrot & Pistachio

TAHINI & FIG

Makes: 12
Preparation: 15 minutes   Chilling: 15 minutes

YOU NEED

75 g unsalted cashews • 75 g dried figs, finely chopped

40 g unsweetened desiccated coconut • 2 tablespoons tahini

1 tablespoon date syrup • 1 teaspoon lemon juice • ½ teaspoon vanilla extract

¼ teaspoon lemon zest • pinch of salt

black and/or white sesame seeds, for rolling

Sesame seeds contain many complex B vitamins that are important of the body, especially the hair, skin and eyes.

B *Brain support* **M** *Mineral rich* **I** *Boosts immunity*

Blitz the cashews, figs and coconut in a food processor until finely ground. Add the tahini, date syrup, lemon juice, vanilla extract, lemon zest and salt. Blitz again until well combined. Using wet hands, shape the dough into 12 balls and roll in the sesame seeds until completely coated. Chill for 15 minutes before serving.

CRANBERRY & ALMOND

Makes: 12
Preparation: 5 minutes   Chilling: 30 minutes

YOU NEED

110 g Medjool dates, pitted • 75 g blanched almonds
50 g dried cranberries • 45 g rolled oats

Almonds are high in calcium, which is great for bone health.

D *Aids digestion* **M** *Mineral rich* **H** *Boosts heart health*

Whizz all of the ingredients in a food processor until the mixture clumps together. Using wet hands, roll the mixture into 12 balls. Chill for 30 minutes before serving.

COCONUT & CASHEW

Makes: 12
Preparation: 10 minutes   Chilling: 30 minutes

YOU NEED

75 g blanched almonds • 75 g cashews • 340 g Medjool dates, pitted
1 tablespoon coconut oil, melted • 40 g unsweetened desiccated coconut

Cashews are high in copper, which is vital for energy production.

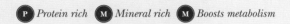 **P** *Protein rich* **M** *Mineral rich* **M** *Boosts metabolism*

Whizz the almonds and cashews in a food processor until finely chopped but not ground. Add the dates and oil and whizz until the mixture clumps together. Using wet hands, roll the mixture into 12 balls, then roll them in desiccated coconut until completely coated. Chill for 30 minutes before serving.

THE ULTIMATE

Makes: 15–20
Preparation: 15 minutes   Chilling: 15 minutes

YOU NEED

115 g blanched almonds • 95 g walnuts • 2 tablespoons ground flaxseeds

2 tablespoons chia seeds • 225 g Medjool dates, pitted

2 tablespoons coconut oil, melted • 1 tablespoon hemp protein powder

1 tablespoon cacao powder • 3 tablespoons almonds, finely chopped

Dates are a great source of fibre, which helps to lower cholesterol. Chia seeds help protect your heart and raw cacao powder stimulates the blood.

D *Aids digestion* **M** *Mineral rich* **B** *Boosts bone health*

Blend the almonds, walnuts, flaxseeds and chia seeds in a food processor for 1 minute. Add all of the remaining ingredients, except the chopped almonds, and blend for another minute until a sticky dough is formed. Using wet hands, roll the mixture into 15–20 balls, then sprinkle the tops with finely chopped almonds. Chill for 15 minutes, until the balls become firm.

BLUEBERRY PALEO

Makes: 12
Preparation: 10 minutes   Chilling: 30 minutes

YOU NEED

55 g coconut flour • 30 g dried blueberries • 3 tablespoons cashew butter (see page 154)
2 tablespoons coconut sugar • ¼ teaspoon ground cinnamon • pinch of salt
230 ml unsweetened almond milk

Dried blueberries are rich in vitamin K, which helps the blood clot properly and plays a crucial role in bone health.

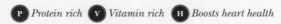 Protein rich V Vitamin rich H Boosts heart health

Put all of the ingredients, except the almond milk, in a bowl and stir until the mixture becomes slightly crumbly. Slowly add the almond milk until it becomes a thick, firm dough. Using wet hands, roll the dough into 12 balls. Chill for at least 30 minutes to firm up.

CINNAMON APPLE

Makes: 8–12
Preparation: 10 minutes   Chilling: 30 minutes

YOU NEED

175 g dried apples • 110 g Medjool dates, pitted
45 g rolled oats • ½ teaspoon ground cinnamon

Dates are high in fibre and B vitamins. They also help to stock up your mineral stores if they get depleted.

B *Brain support*   **M** *Mineral rich*   **I** *Boosts immunity*

Combine all of the ingredients in a food processor and whizz until it forms a thick paste. Roll into 8 balls, using 1 tablespoon of mixture for each ball. If you want to make more, roll into 12 balls, using 1 teaspoon of mixture for each ball. Chill for 30 minutes before serving.

CACAO CHIA COCONUT

Makes: 12
Preparation: 10 minutes   Chilling: 30 minutes

YOU NEED
50 g natural smooth peanut butter (see page 154)

75 g honey (preferably raw) • ½ teaspoon ground cinnamon

¼ teaspoon salt • 130 g rolled oats • 40 g chia seeds

20 g unsweetened desiccated coconut • 40 g ground flaxseeds

1 tablespoon cacao nibs

These energy balls are full of protein, which keeps you feeling fuller for longer.

D *Aids digestion* **V** *Vitamin rich* **S** *Improves skin*

Whisk the peanut butter and honey together in a bowl until smooth. Stir in the cinnamon and salt. Add the oats, chia seeds, coconut and flaxseeds and stir until well combined. Stir in the cacao nibs then, using wet hands, roll the mixture into 12 balls. Chill for 30 minutes before serving.

FIG & WALNUT

Makes: 12
Preparation: 15 minutes   Chilling: 15 minutes

YOU NEED

450 g dried figs, hard stems removed • 125 g walnut halves

40 g ground flaxseeds • 1 tablespoon vanilla extract • ½ teaspoon salt

High-fibre ingredients like figs will keep you satisfied for longer. They also contain prebiotics to help support the pre-existing good bacteria in the gut.

D *Aids digestion*   **V** *Vitamin rich*   **B** *Bone strengthening*

Pulse all of the ingredients in a food processor for about 4 minutes until finely chopped and almost a sand consistency. Scoop out the mixture with a tablespoon and, using wet hands, form into 12 balls. Chill for 15 minutes to firm up.

ALMOND & CAROB

Makes: 12
Preparation: 15 minutes   Chilling: 15 minutes

YOU NEED

150 g blanched almonds • 25 g carob chips • 75 g unsweetened desiccated coconut
300 g Medjool dates, pitted • 1 tablespoon coconut oil, melted

Carob improves digestion and lowers cholesterol levels in the blood. It is also used for treating diarrhoea in both children and adults.

D *Aids digestion*   **P** *Protein rich*   **M** *Mineral rich*

Blitz the almonds, carob chips and coconut in a food processor until finely ground. Add the dates, oil and 2 tablespoons of water and pulse until it forms a dough. Using wet hands, roll the dough into 12 balls. Chill for 15 minutes.

CRANBERRY & ORANGE

Makes: 18
Preparation: 10 minutes   Chilling: 30 minutes

YOU NEED

240 g Medjool dates, pitted and roughly chopped • 70 g dried cranberries
30 g vanilla whey protein powder + extra for rolling • 65 g flaked almonds
1½ teaspoons orange zest • 2 teaspoons coconut oil, melted

Dates and cranberries are high in fibre, which helps maintain bowel health.

P *Protein rich* **V** *Vitamin rich* **B** *Blood building*

Whizz the dates and cranberries in a food processor until crumbly. Add the protein powder, almonds and orange zest and whizz until well combined. With the processor running, slowly add the oil in a steady stream until the mixture forms a sticky ball. Pour some extra vanilla protein powder onto a plate. Using wet hands, shape the mixture into 12 balls, using a tablespoon of mixture for each ball. Roll each ball in the protein powder until coated. Shake off any excess. Chill for 30 minutes.

SPICED PUMPKIN

Makes: 12
Preparation: 40 minutes   Chilling: 30 minutes   Freezing: 15 minutes

YOU NEED
110 g Pumpkin Purée (see page 156) • 120 g almond butter (see page 154)
85 g pure maple syrup • ½ teaspoon ground cinnamon + 1 tablespoon for topping
½ teaspoon allspice • 115 g rolled oats • 45 g pumpkin seeds
50 g raisins • 2 tablespoons chia seeds

Pumpkin is packed with vitamin A, which helps improve vision.

B *Blood building* **V** *Vitamin rich* **B** *Body strengthening*

Put the pumpkin, almond butter, maple syrup and spices in a bowl and stir until smooth. Fold in the oats, pumpkin seeds, raisins and chia seeds. Cover and chill for 30 minutes to firm up. Roll the mixture into 12 balls, then sprinkle them with cinnamon. Freeze for 15 minutes to firm up. Defrost for a few minutes before eating.

MATCHA CHOCOLATE

Makes: 10
Preparation: 15 minutes   Chilling: 15 minutes

YOU NEED

110 g Medjool dates, pitted • 75 g blanched almonds • 35 g cacao powder
1 tablespoon matcha green tea powder + extra for dusting
1 tablespoon unsweetened almond milk

Matcha green tea powder is full of antioxidants to boost metabolism and burn calories. It also enhances mood and aids concentration.

D *Aids digestion*　**P** *Protein rich*　**M** *Mineral rich*

Blend the dates and almonds in a food processor until they come together and form a sticky ball. Break the ball up and add the cacao powder, matcha powder and almond milk. Pulse until all the ingredients are combined. Roll into 10 small balls and dust with more matcha powder. Chill for 15 minutes before serving.

GOLDEN SULTANA & COCONUT

Makes: 12
Preparation: 15 minutes   Chilling: 20 minutes

YOU NEED

150 g golden sultanas • 75 g hazelnuts • 55 g rolled oats

2 tablespoons ground flaxseeds • 1 tablespoon honey (preferably raw)

¼ teaspoon vanilla extract • pinch of salt • 75 g coconut flakes, toasted

Golden raisins contain the flavonoid quercetin, which may benefit those with allergies. It has antihistamine and anti-inflammatory properties.

M *Mineral rich* **I** *Boosts immunity* **B** *Body strengthening*

Put the sultanas into a bowl, cover with hot water and leave for 5 minutes, then pat dry.
Blend the hazelnuts, oats and flaxseeds in a food processor until finely ground.
Add the sultanas, honey, vanilla extract and salt and pulse until a sticky ball forms.
Using wet hands, roll the mixture into 12 small balls, then sprinkle the tops with
toasted coconut flakes. Chill for 20 minutes before serving.

DATE & NUT BUTTER

Makes: 22
Preparation: 20 minutes   Chilling: 15 minutes

YOU NEED

60 g almond butter (see page 154) • 60 g cashew butter (see page 154)

350 g Medjool dates, pitted and chopped

150 g blanched almonds • 60 g walnuts

1 teaspoon vanilla extract • sea salt, for topping

Cashews promote heart health and are also have a high copper content, which is vital for energy production.

P *Protein rich* **B** *Brain support* **V** *Vitamin rich*

Heat the nut butters in a pan for 20 seconds. Blitz the dates, almonds and walnuts in a food processor until there are no large chunks. Add the nut butters and whizz until smooth. Add the vanilla and pulse a few times to combine. Roll the mixture into 22 small balls, using a tablespoon of mixture for each ball. Sprinkle with sea salt, place onto a baking sheet and chill for 15 minutes.

ALMOND & QUINOA

Makes: about 36
Preparation: 10 minutes   Chilling: 15 minutes

YOU NEED

170 g red quinoa, cooked • 120 g almond butter (see page 154)
110 g honey (preferably raw) • 85 g ground flaxseeds
45 g dried plums, roughly chopped • 30 g goji berries • 1 teaspoon vanilla extract

Red quinoa has the highest protein content of all grains. It also contains a quarter of your recommended daily intake of zinc, essential for a healthy immune system.

P *Protein rich* **M** *Mineral rich* **D** *Aids digestion*

Put all of the ingredients into a bowl and stir until well combined. Using wet hands, roll the mixture into about 36 small balls, then chill for 15 minutes to firm up.

LEMON CHIA CASHEW

Makes: 12
Preparation: 15 minutes   Chilling: 10 minutes

YOU NEED

150 g cashews • 45 g rolled oats • 35 g raw coconut flakes + extra for topping
pinch of salt • 200 g Medjool dates, pitted
2 tablespoons chia seeds • zest of 1 lemon

Cashews are rich in magnesium, which is thought to improve recall and delay age-related memory loss.

B *Brain support* **M** *Mineral rich* **B** *Blood building*

Pulse the cashews, oats, coconut and salt in a food processor until finely ground. Add the dates, 60 ml of hot water, chia seeds and lemon zest and pulse until the mixture forms a dough. Using wet hands, roll the mixture into 12 balls, then sprinkle with coconut flakes. Chill for 10 minutes to firm up.

SPICED OATS & ACAI

Makes: 24
Preparation: 15 minutes   Chilling: 15 minutes

YOU NEED

140 g dried cranberries • 2 tablespoons vanilla whey protein powder
85 g rolled oats • 2 teaspoons ground cinnamon
acai powder, for dusting

Acai berries contain antioxidants, fibre and heart-healthy fats. They are also rich in calcium, iron and vitamin E.

P *Protein rich* **M** *Mineral rich* **D** *Aids digestion*

Put the cranberries in a heatproof bowl, cover with hot water and leave for 1 minute. Drain and add to a food processor with 1 tablespoon of water. Pulse until smooth. Combine the protein powder, oats and cinnamon in a bowl and stir in the cranberry paste, adding 1–3 teaspoons of water if needed. Using wet hands, roll the mixture into 24 balls, then sprinkle the acai powder on top. Chill for 15 minutes.

CHIA & CHERRY

Makes: 12
Preparation: 10 minutes   Chilling: 30 minutes

YOU NEED

75 g blanched almonds • 35 g cashews, ground • 55 g Medjool dates, pitted
30 g vanilla whey protein powder • 120 g dried cherries
2 tablespoons chia seeds • 2 tablespoons almond butter (see page 154)
1 tablespoon pure maple syrup • 1 teaspoon vanilla extract
½ teaspoon almond extract • 30 g cacao nibs

Dried cherries are a good source of copper, which aids collagen production. This process keeps your tissues strong.

B *Blood building* **M** *Mineral rich* **I** *Boosts immunity*

Whizz the almonds, cashews, dates and protein powder in a food processor until finely chopped and well combined. Add the remaining ingredients, except the cacao nibs and 40 g of the dried cherries, and whizz for 1–2 minutes, until a dough starts to form. Roughly chop the remaining dried cherries and fold them into the mixture with the cacao nibs. Using wet hands, roll the mixture into 12 balls. Chill for 30 minutes.

APRICOT & CASHEW

Makes: 24
Preparation: 15 minutes   Chilling: 15 minutes

YOU NEED

60 g cashews, toasted • 20 g sesame seeds, toasted • 80 g dried apricots
20 g puffed brown rice • thumb-sized piece of ginger, peeled and grated
½ teaspoon mixed spice • 2 tablespoons honey (preferably raw)
40 g ground cashews, for dusting

Apricots are high in potassium, which help cells in the body function p... are also great for heart function and muscle contraction.

B *Brain support*   **I** *Boosts immunity*   **V** *Vitamin rich*

Blitz the cashews, sesame seeds, apricots and brown rice in a food processor until finely chopped. Add the ginger, mixed spice and honey and blitz again for 1–2 minutes. Using wet hands, roll the mixture into 24 small balls, rolling them in the ground cashews. Shake to remove any excess. Chill for 15 minutes to firm up.

COCONUT

Makes: 8
Preparation: 10 minutes   Chilling: 15 minutes

YOU NEED

1½ teaspoons unsweetened almond milk • 50 g unsweetened desiccated coconut

2 tablespoons coconut butter, melted • 1 tablespoon coconut oil, melted

1 tablespoon agave nectar

Coconut is antiviral, antibacterial, and boosts the immune system. It also helps the body to absorb calcium, which is great for healthy bones.

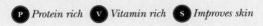 *Protein rich* *Vitamin rich* *Improves skin*

Mix the milk and coconut together in a bowl and leave for a minute. Add the remaining ingredients and stir until well combined. Using wet hands, roll the mixture into 8 balls. Chill for 15 minutes to firm up.

COCONUT & DATE

Makes: 12
Preparation: 10 minutes   Chilling: 10 minutes

YOU NEED

50 g cashews • 250 g Medjool dates, pitted

40 g unsweetened desiccated coconut • 1 tablespoon coconut oil, melted

Dates are high in fibre and eating them does not spike blood sugar levels.

 **E** *Boosts energy* **P** *Protein rich* **M** *Mineral rich*

Blitz the cashews in a food processor for 10 seconds. Add the dates, 20 g of the
coconut, the oil and 1 tablespoon of water and blitz for another minute. Using wet
hands, shape the mixture into 12 balls, then roll them in the remaining coconut.
Chill for 10 minutes to firm up.

CRANBERRY & POMEGRANATE

Makes: 12
Preparation: 15 minutes   Chilling: 30 minutes

YOU NEED

100 g dried cranberries • 85 g rolled oats • 80 g ground flaxseeds
75 g blanched almonds • 2 tablespoons honey (preferably raw)
½ pomegranate, seeds only

Pomegranate seeds are a good source of vitamins C and K. Vitamin C enhances iron absorption whereas K is important in maintaining strong, healthy bones.

D *Aids digestion*　**V** *Vitamin rich*　**B** *Body strengthening*

Whizz the cranberries, oats, flaxseeds, almonds and honey in a food processor until they form a paste. Dry the pomegranate seeds on paper towels. Using a tablespoon of mixture for each ball, roll the mixture into 12 balls, pushing some of the pomegranate seeds into each one. Chill for 30 minutes.

LEMON & POPPY SEED

Makes: 14
Preparation: 10 minutes   Chilling: 15 minutes

YOU NEED

25 g rolled oats • 45 g vanilla whey protein powder
1 tablespoon poppy seeds + 2 tablespoons for topping • 45 ml lemon juice
1 teaspoon lemon zest

Poppy seeds are a great source of minerals including calcium, iron and zinc.

P *Protein rich*   **M** *Mineral rich*   **I** *Boosts immunity*

Put the oats, protein powder and poppy seeds into a bowl and stir. Add the lemon
juice and zest and 45 ml of water and stir until fully combined. Using wet hands, roll
the mixture into 14 small balls, then dip each ball in the remaining poppy seeds.
Chill for 15 minutes to firm up.

PUFFED ALMOND

Makes: 7
Preparation: 10 minutes   Freezing: 5 minutes

YOU NEED

60 g almond butter (see page 154) • 3 tablespoons brown rice syrup

1 teaspoon vanilla extract • 25 g puffed brown rice

1 tablespoon cacao nibs

Almonds are a great source of calcium, which is good for bones and teeth.

 **P** *Protein rich* **V** *Vitamin rich* **I** *Boosts immunity*

Melt the nut butter, rice syrup and vanilla extract together and stir to combine. Add the remaining ingredients to the bowl and stir until thoroughly mixed. Using wet hands, roll the mixture into 7 balls, then freeze for 5 minutes. These balls can stay in the freezer until needed. Defrost before eating.

SPICED CARROT & PISTACHIO

Makes: 12
Preparation: 15 minutes   Chilling: 1 hour

YOU NEED

100 g porridge oats • 75 g raisins • 25 g carrot, grated • 1 teaspoon vanilla extract
1 teaspoon ground cinnamon • ½ teaspoon nutmeg, grated
¼ teaspoon ground ginger • 175 g Medjool dates, pitted
25 g pistachios, finely ground, for dusting

Pistachios contain more protein than any other nut. They are a great source of monounsaturated fatty acids.

P *Protein rich*　**M** *Mineral rich*　**V** *Vitamin rich*

Blitz the oats and raisins in a food processor for a few seconds. Add the carrots, vanilla and spices and blitz again. Add the dates and 65 ml of water and blitz again until it forms a sticky dough. Using wet hands, shape the dough into 12 balls, then dust or roll in the ground pistachios. Chill for 1 hour to firm up.

BUTTERS & PURÉES

*Here are a few handy recipes to help you
make the seed and nut butters and purées
that are used in the bars and balls. They
will give you a good boost of protein,
helping you to feel fuller for longer.*

Cinnamon Pumpkin Seed Butter • Date Purée
Home-made Nut & Seed Butters
Pumpkin Purée

CINNAMON PUMPKIN SEED BUTTER

Makes: 400 g
Preparation: 10 minutes   Cooking: 15 minutes

YOU NEED
¼ teaspoon ground cinnamon • 400 g pumpkin seeds
1½ tablespoons pure maple syrup

Pumpkin seeds are the only seed that is alkaline-forming, helping to balance the pH of the body. They are a great source of vitamin K, all the B vitamins and zinc.

P *Protein rich*   **M** *Mineral rich*   **A** *Alkalising*

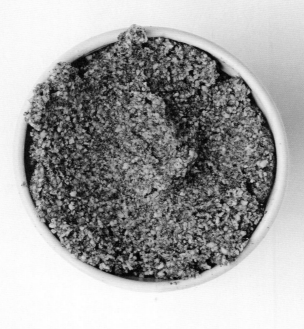

Preheat the oven to 180°C (350°F/Gas 4). Mix the cinnamon and pumpkin seeds together. Spread them out onto a baking sheet and bake for 15 minutes, then leave to cool. Whizz in a food processor, scraping down the sides with a spatula from time to time. Once the mixture forms a ball, add the maple syrup and whizz to a purée. Store in an airtight container for up to a week.

DATE PURÉE

Makes: 450 g
Preparation: 10 minutes + 20 minutes soaking

YOU NEED

450 g Medjool dates, pitted • 1 tablespoon lemon juice
½ teaspoon grated lemon zest

Dates are full of fibre, which helps you to feel fuller for longer.

D *Aids digestion* **M** *Mineral rich* **E** *Boosts energy*

Put the dates into a heatproof bowl and pour in 235 ml of boiling water. Soak for 20 minutes, or until dates have softened. Pour the dates and their soaking water into a food processor, add the lemon juice and zest and blend until smooth. Store in the fridge for up to a week.

HOME-MADE NUT & SEED BUTTERS

Makes: 300 g
Preparation: 5 minutes

YOU NEED

300 g nuts* or seeds of your choice • 4 tablespoons coconut oil, melted

* When choosing the nuts, make sure they are roasted or toasted and unsalted.

Nuts are high in protein, which helps to keep hunger at bay.

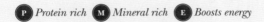 **P** *Protein rich* **M** *Mineral rich* **E** *Boosts energy*

Blend all of the ingredients in a food processor until they form a smooth butter.
Store in an airtight jar or container for up to a week.

PUMPKIN PURÉE

Makes: 350 g
Preparation: 15 minutes   Cooking: 20 minutes

YOU NEED

¼ pumpkin, peeled and cut into chunks

Pumpkins are full of vitamin C, which helps build your immune system. They are also rich in fibre, which helps keep you fuller for longer.

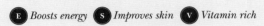 **E** *Boosts energy*   **S** *Improves skin*   **V** *Vitamin rich*

Put the pumpkin in a large pan and cover with water. Bring to the boil, then reduce the heat and simmer for 20 minutes. Drain, add to the food processor and blitz until smooth. Store in the fridge for up to 3 days.

INDEX

Acknowledgements

Thanks so much to Kathy Steer and Alice Chadwick for all their work on this
Green Series and in particular *Energy Bars & Balls*. Thank you Poppy Mahon for
her brilliant assistance. Deirdre Rooney, thank you for your endless support and
fabulous photography.

Energy Bars & Balls by Fern Green

First published in 2016 by Hachette Books
(Marabout)
This English hardback edition published in 2017
by Hardie Grant Books, an imprint of Hardie
Grant Publishing

Hardie Grant Books (UK)
52-54 Southwark Street
London SE1 1UN

Hardie Grant Books (Australia)
Ground Floor, Building 1
658 Church Street
Melbourne, VIC 3121

hardiegrantbooks.com

The moral rights of Fern Green to be
identified as the author of this work have
been asserted by her in accordance with the
Copyright, Designs and Patents Act 1988.

Text © Fern Green
Photography © Deirdre Rooney

British Library Cataloguing-in-Publication Data.
A catalogue record for this book is available
from the British Library.

ISBN: 978-1-78488-104-7

Publisher: Catie Ziller
Editor: Kathy Steer
Designer & illustrator: Alice Chadwick
Author: Fern Green
Photographer: Deirdre Rooney

For the English hardback edition:
Publisher: Kate Pollard
Senior Editor: Kajal Mistry
Editorial Assistant: Hannah Roberts
Proofreader: Jessica Gooch
Colour Reproduction by p2d

Printed and bound in China by Leo Paper
Group